I KNOW THEE BY NAME

How to Get Closer to God in 90 Days

Victor Scott Rodriguez

VSR Publishing

New York

ACKNOWLEDGMENTS

I have already co-written a singles guide and a romantic comedy trilogy. The Metropolicks trilogy definitely has religious/spiritual elements to the storyline, however, they are not books that would be placed in the religion section of a bookstore. This is not only my first solo writing experience, it is also my first venture into doing a book that falls into the inspiration category. But God willing, it will not be my last inspiration book.

Of special thanks are those that led me to a saving knowledge of God and an early foundation in the Bible. This includes: Billy Graham, Hal Lindsey, David Wilkerson, Joni Eareckson Tada, Evie Karlsson, George Beverly Shea, Donald R. Hubbard, Stephen F. Olford, Erwin W. Lutzer, Philip Yancey and Dick Eastman. Also I want to especially thank my great grandmother Golda (Bubbie) for her incredible stories of faith from the "old country." A big debt of thanks goes to my mother, Diane G. Rodriguez, who always believed in me and stuck by me through thick and thin. I also owe a huge debt of gratitude to Rev. Floyd Knight, Jr., who has been a close friend for more than twenty years. Much gratitude also goes to Kerrick Thomas and Nelson Searcy of the Journey Church in New York City. I have gone to the Journey Church for more than a decade and their support has been invaluable.

Thanks to Gilly Rosenthol who formatted this book and has helped through multiple time sensitive deadlines. Thanks to IP attorney Rob Thony for his help. And last but not least, thanks to Rebecca Jackson for her love and support.

Victor

INTRODUCTION

The number 40 in the Bible is always significant. The number forty is associated with trouble, hardship, trials, tribulations, testing, endurance and God's judgement. It is not a "happy" number. It is associated with tests of faith that then develop one's moral and spiritual character. Many times we say we are devoted to God, but testing that involves "forty days and forty nights" or forty years signifies a rising above our shortcomings.

I became a believer at the age of 17 years old. I wish I could say that it was smooth sailing and uphill the entire time.

However, for the past 40 years (yes I really am that old) I have been at times a carnal believer or even a backslidden believer. So much so that I really identify with the story of the prodigal son in the Bible. But after 40 years of experience I can honestly say that I have learned some things. Some "tricks of the trade" so to speak. So after 4 decades of walking with God, the thought came to me of writing books that would share what I have learned. I recently saw *Star Wars: The Last Jedi* and was encouraged to see the character of Yoda telling Luke yet again to "pass on what you have learned." Not that I am in any way an expert. But similar to Luke in that movie, I feel that even those of us who identify with the elder Luke's feelings of weakness and failure can still pass on the lessons we have learned. So how to do that?

Multiple studies show that 90 days consistently applied makes a permanent habit of some practice. In 12 step programs the motto is "90 meetings in 90 days", because it has been proven by experience that 90 days is the minimum needed to break out of a bad habit and create a permanent new habit. So for the next 90 days (the equivalent of 13 weeks) I encourage you to read the chapters in this book to help you to develop a closer walk with God.

The bible verses that I have chosen are specific to helping those of you who are asking the question of "Why God?", or are struggling with feeling abandoned by God, or are overwhelmed by life's problems. Life is hard and Jesus told us that we are to take up our cross daily. So for the next 90 days I encourage to take this journey with me as we explore what the Bible has to say in response to those questions.

WEEK ONE

"And the Lord said unto Moses, I will do this thing also that thou hast spoken: for thou hast found grace in my sight, and I know thee by name."

Exodus 33:7

We begin this 90 day book with looking at our key verse for the entire book. In the book of Exodus God reveals himself to Moses initially at the Burning Bush. Then multiple times God communicates to Moses as he instructs him how to deliver the Israelites out of bondage. Then in Exodus chapter 33 God tells Moses that "I know thee by name" in response to Moses wanting to know that God will be with him as he leads the Israelites to the promised land.

But what is significant in this verse is that God is telling Moses what he also wants to tell to you and I. That we are known by God by our name. That even though God promised Abraham that his offspring would be as numerous as the grains of sand, that each of us is known to God. That we are not just a number. That we are not just grains of sand on the beach. That each and every person is important and special to God. In Matthew chapter 10, Jesus says that God knows the exact numbers of hairs on your head.

So let day one and week one of this journey be a reminder that you are of infinite worth to God. You are important to God. He made you to be in close relationship with him. The only hindrance to that happening is your own free will, or rather you lack of willingness. So let's get started as we examine the other bible verses to get to a closer walk with God.

WEEK TWO

"...Not by might, nor by power, but by my Spirit, says the Lord of Hosts."

Zechariah 4:6

The pressures and stresses of daily life can seem overwhelming at times. It is a rat race and the rats sometimes seem to be winning. In our own power, life can definitely feel like a lose/lose situation. However, God does not ask us to face life by ourselves. God wants to become involved in our lives. He wants us to invite him to take part in our daily struggles and seek his power to achieve our goals. God created a world of free will and even he must respect those boundaries and limitations. He cannot force himself on someone. He invites, he reaches out in subtle ways, he whispers in a still small voice and he waits for us to respond. God many times gives us more than we can handle in our own power deliberately, so that we can reach out to him to give us the strength that we do not possess. Do not try to do it all on your own. Allow God's Holy Spirit to work through you. It involves an element of surrender and I know that is very hard. But the reward for living in God's power is worth it.

WEEK THREE

"But my God shall supply all your need according to his riches in glory by Christ Jesus."

Philippians 4:19

In 2008 the entire world was hit by a financial crisis. Movies like *The Big Short* try to explain what happened. But the reality of the situation is that it was caused by sheer greed and irresponsibility on the part of Wall Street.

Millions of people were affected as people lost jobs and lost their savings. We live in a world of uncertainty. The TV show *Two Broke Girls* illustrates how tough it is as many people live paycheck to paycheck. Money is a huge stressor in our lives. Or rather, the lack of money. But God says that he essentially has that covered. Jehovah Jirah means God will provide in Hebrew.

God doesn't say in the Bible that we will have all our wants met, but that we will have our "needs" met. We many times live beyond our means and more times than not it is a situation of our spending that causes money stresses, instead of what we are not earning. The Apostle Paul learned to live in all circumstances. The Israelites as they wandered in the desert had manna every day. They eventually got tired of the daily manna and complained repeatedly to his servant Moses. When they complained of a lack of meat, God provided them with quail. God did provide, but not to their liking. That is usually the situation with all of us as well. Let us learn to be grateful for the glass that is half full instead of looking for what is missing.

WEEK FOUR

"O my Lord, send, I pray thee, by the hand of him whom thou wilt send."

Exodus 4: 13

Moses was brought up as a Prince of Egypt. He enjoyed the lavish lifestyle of being royalty. Then at the age of 40 years old, he intervened when he saw a hebrew slave being whipped and killed the Egyptian overseer. When he found out that his murder was known, he ran to the wilderness, eventually finding rest in the tent of Jethro. Then for the next 40 years of his life he was a shepherd. From royalty to sheep herder had to be a big blow to his ego and pride. So the 80 year old shepherd was very different from the 40 year old prince. It is to the 80 year old that God appears in a burning bush. As an old man now he has given up his dreams of being a leader.

So when God appears to him and tells him that he has been chosen to lead the Israelites out of bondage, Moses does not respond with any version of enthusiasm. In fact, he gave excuse after excuse why he was not the man for the job. Finally after every excuse had been countered by God, Moses said essentially that God should send someone else. Only at this point does God get angry at Moses. None of his prior excuses were met by God's anger. So why did Moses' refusal cause a different reaction in God?

Because God can work with human nature. He can work with our weakness. He knows that we are weak. God knows that we will fail. But the one thing God will not override is our free will. He created a system where we have choice. God told Moses that Aaron would be his helper, his mouthpiece.

Moses at 80 years old now had the self-image of a failure. The confidence of the 40 year old prince was gone. He only saw his shortcomings and the fact that he was a stutterer. But God does not care about our shortcomings. It has been said that God is more concerned about our availability, instead of our abilities.

Sometimes he picks people deliberately so that they would need to rely on him for their success. So to speak to Pharoah and the nation of Egypt, God picked a man who is "slow of speech",as Moses describes himself. Let us not let our short-coming prevent us from the task that God has set before us.

WEEK FIVE

"Henceforth I call you not servants; for the servant knoweth not what his lord doeth: but I have called you friends; for all things that I have heard from my Father I have made known to you."

John 15:15

The Christian faith is unique among the religions of the world in that we are allowed a unique and special relationship to the King of the Universe. Christianity is more about a relationship with God, than a religion. There are only two people in the Bible that are so close to God, that he refers to them as his "friend." Abraham, who is considered the first Jewish person and the patriarch of the Hebrew lineage, is called a friend of God in several verses of the Bible. In Exodus chapter 33, verse 11; it says "And God spake to Moses face to face, as a man speakest unto his friend."

But then in chapter 15 of the Gospel of John, all of the apostles are called friends of God. And Jesus' words later in that book make it clear that all of his followers are considered his friends, and no longer servants. Think about that. Having the Lord God Almighty as your personal friend. But most believers do not think that way. They many times view

God as distant and hard to approach. But the simple truth is that you can talk to God anytime, anywhere and under any circumstances. He is just waiting for you to respond. He has already reached out to you through Jesus Christ. The next move is on you.

WEEK SIX

"Thou shalt have no other gods before me."

Exodus 20:3

When God gave Moses the 10 Commandments on Mount Sinai, the very 1st commandment was to not have any other "gods." In ancient times, that meant bowing down to statues of "gods" made out of stone or wood and praying to them for your needs. There were many gods in the world of 1250 BC, which is approximately when Moses received the two tablets of stone engraved by "the finger of God." So this commandment was pretty straightforward for its time. There was a god for this and a god for that. You had to know which god to go to for your every need or problem. The concept of one all powerful God was unheard of. In modern terminology, that would be like "a one-stop shop" for all your prayers.

But God's definition of "other gods" was and is much more expansive. A "god" can be anything or any person which is placed in a higher value than God. God literally wants to be first place in everyone's life. I have found that out the hard way over the past few decades. It could be a career, a prospective girlfriend, a friend, a residence, or anything else that you or

I place in higher value than our relation-ship with him. When you want it so badly that it becomes the most important thing in your life, it becomes an idol.

The Bible says that in Exodus 20 that "for I the Lord thy God am a jealous God" and I really believe him. Idols in my life have disappeared repeatedly until I finally got the message. Put him first. So I highly encourage you to look at your life and figure out if there is anything or anyone who is more important to you than God.

WEEK SEVEN

---

*"He must increase, but
I must decrease."*

John 3:30

The religious leaders in Israel in the Gospel of John wanted to know who John The Baptist claimed to be.

John The Baptist responded that he was a voice "crying out in the wilderness." His job was to prepare the way for the Messiah. To preach a message of repentance to the masses in Israel and prepare their hearts to be ready for Jesus.

When his followers were jealous that crowds were now going to Jesus, John The Baptist responded that "a man can receive nothing, except it be given him from heaven."

Meaning that he knew his place and his purpose. It was as a herald of the Messiah, not to be the Messiah. But there was a more important truth in that he knew that Jesus' ministry needed to increase as his in turn began to decrease. That it was not a competition. That he was not a self-promoter, but was instead a God-promoter.

Each of us should look at our own lives to see if we are being God-promoters. I had a friend once who said that "well, we are all self-centered to some extent." I told her that was true, but that there were levels of being self-centered. Some people are more self-centered than others. Especially where I live, New York City, there is an emphasis on being self-focused. However, that is definitely not God's will. He wants all of us to be thinking about ways to make his light shine, instead of our own.

He is looking for people who want to hold his name up high.

WEEK EIGHT

"Dave said moreover, The Lord that delivered me out of the paw of the lion, and out of the paw of the bear, he will deliver me out of the hand of this Philistine."

1 Samuel 17:37

The story of David and Goliath is one of the most famous stories in the Bible. The giant Goliath came out against the entire army of Israel, under King Saul. Goliath put forth a challenge for a one on one fight to the death between him and any soldier in Israel, to determine who would win the battle between the Philistines and Israel. David, the teenager who was a shepherd, heard Goliath's taunts and went to King Saul to ask to fight for Israel. Saul looked at the little teenager and thought he was joking. How could a young man with no military fighting go against a giant over 9 feet tall who scared every soldier in Israel's army?

But David responded that even though he had no military training, he was not untrained. He had spent years guarding his father's flock. Whenever a lion or a bear would try to grab one of the sheep, David did not run away. Instead he went after the wild animal with a club and hit it until the sheep was free. He demonstrated courage repeatedly against foes stronger than him. He did not think he did this on his own. He gave credit to God. So when he went out against Goliath with a slingshot and a stone, the giant laughed at him initially. That is until the stone was thrown into Goliath's forehead and he fell to the ground.

For you and I, when we face the giants in our life, we need to remember the times when God delivered us from past enemies and troubles. For most of us believers, we can remember when God has come through for us during a crisis. That is the message of this bible verse. To know that God who delivered you from your past problems, can now deliver you for this present problem. I know that this current problem can seem so big that it resembles

Goliath. But God will be with you just like he was with the young shepherd boy.

WEEK NINE

"Therefore I take pleasure in infirmities, in reproaches, in necessities, in persecutions, in distresses for Christ's sake: for when I am weak, then I am strong."

2 Corinthians 12: 10

Of all the verses in the Bible, this one is my personal favorite. I have always viewed myself as weak. I have had multiple health issues throughout my life. In 2007, I was in the intensive cardiac care unit of the Lenox Hill hospital in Manhattan. The nurses nicknamed me "Walkie Talkie" because I was the only person in the ward that was not in a coma, and that could walk and talk. From my early childhood in school I was never the athletic type. I was the nerd in high school, not the jock. So this verse always had an appeal to me.

But this verse originally was applied to the apostle Paul who was suffering from what he called the "thorn in the flesh." Scholars have attempted to guess what the "thorn" or affliction was, but no one knows for sure. He was stoned so many times that it could be any physical ailment. Some guess that it was his eyesight and others think it might be physical pain. Some even theorize that it was lust since he was single.

But the point of the verse is that God was telling Paul that God's strength is perfected in weakness. That he uses areas of our life where we feel inadequate to demonstrate his power. Case in point is Gideon in the book of Judges, chapter 7. Gideon was going to battle and yet God by different tests whittled down the army to just 300. Since from God's perspective a large army might credit themselves with the victory, but an army of 300 would have to give credit to God. God chose Moses, a stutterer, to be his spokesperson. He chose a teenage shepherd boy to face a giant. He chose Paul who was trained as a Jewish scholar, not to speak to the Jews, but instead, to speak to the Gentiles.

Something he was totally untrained for. This is how God operates. The sooner you learn it, the sooner God will be able to start demonstrating his power in your life.

WEEK TEN

*"Be still, and know
that I am God."*

Psalm 46:10

How many times in an argument do you find yourself thinking of how to respond, instead of actually listening to what the other person is trying to say? I have attended classes on active listening. It is hard to really listen to a person and truly hear them. Most of the time in this fast paced world, we are thinking of other things and our mind is distracted, even when we are engaged in conversation.

To be in relationship with God, you need to understand that God gives each of us free will. He will not normally override that to get our attention. Aside from miracles in the Bible, such as Saul of Tarsus having a Damascus Road experience or Balaam having his donkey talk to him, God is usually very low-key in how he talks to humans. To really hear God involves something that few of us are every good at. To be blunt it involves shutting up.

In 1 Kings chapter 19, God speaks to the prophet Elijah by means of his "still small voice." In other words, God whispered to Elijah. We think that God always communicates in a loud, booming voice. However, that is not what the Bible says. To really hear God's voice, you need to quiet your mind and truly listen.

I have heard God's voice only once. I was torn as to which graduate school to go to. Somehow I felt that my entire future would be decided by this decision. That I was at a crossroads in my life. God literally whispered the words "go to Chicago" and as a result I accepted the invitation to go to the University of Chicago Divinity School. I received a master of arts in divinity degree there but then two years later I was not accepted into their Ph.d. program. If I had gone to another school I would have been accepted into the Ph.d. program upon acceptance and would now be a professor. There were other schools where I could of gone to continue as a Ph.d. student, but I felt that God had closed that door. That it was not God's will. After that I began a career in the public sector. Of all the many decisions I have made in life, I often wonder why did I hear that whisper for that decision. But the decision to go to Chicago changed the trajectory of my life.

In a similar way, I encourage you to quiet yourself, be still and listen for God's still small voice of a whisper. He will guide you to give you a future and a hope.

WEEK ELEVEN

*"I am made all things to
all men, that I might by
all means save some."*

1 Corinthians 9:22

One of the reasons why I like the Journey church in New York City so much is that they are very open to new approaches to communicate the gospel. They do what they call "servant evangelism" where they hand out granola bars or bottles of water with a postcard advertising the church. They do multimedia montages and movie clips for the church services and play contemporary christian music at every church service. In today's modern world, it is important to try new approaches to communicate the gospel. To get the gospel out by being all things to all people.

However, this idea of being current with the gospel message has always been the case for centuries. When Handel's *Messiah* originally was performed, the audiences viewed it as scandalous. Church leaders were initially negative about contemporary christian music when it became popular in the 1970's. Mel Gibson's *The Passion of the Christ* was viewed by some as too violent. Roma Downey and Mark Burnett's *The Bible* were criticized for using a sexy Portuguese model as Jesus Christ.

When I co-wrote the romantic comedy Metropolicks trilogy, my pastors Nelson Searcy, Kerrick Thomas and Kerrick's wife Lorie; gave me legal consent to be in the books as themselves. The Journey church is a major part of the storyline of the trilogy. While not "christian books", the trilogy has a storyline of a modern day prodigal son story and also a storyline of a virgin growth group (small bible study) leader who struggles to stay pure in New York City. The books are definitely R-rated and yet when the pastors read the books, they said that as long as the books promoted the gospel, that they would be okay with it.

To me that is what the church has always done. Made the message of the gospel relevant to every audience. When DC Talk came out as the first popular Christian rap group, even I was initially hesitant. But now I can say that I love their songs. So when you communicate the gospel to your friends, do not have blinders on. Figure out what is the best way to communicate what you believe and maybe try a new method or means of communicating. Literally let God, not people, be the judge of your effectiveness.

WEEK TWELVE

"And he called unto him his disciples, and saith unto them, Verily I say to you, That this poor widow hath cast more in, than all they which have cast into the treasury..."

Mark 12: 43

The story of the widow's mite is one of my favorites in the Bible. Jesus uses her contribution to the treasury as an example of how he views each of our contributions. The moral of the story is that God looks at the quality of what we do, not the quantity. God says there is a big difference if you are a billionaire and you contribute $10,000 to a charity; as compared to a poor widow who lives on her social security check contributing the same $10,000. Jesus says that the rich person contributed out "of their abundance" and yet the widow gave "all that she had."

This applies to all areas of our life. Quality counts in everything with God. The quality of our time versus the quantity of our time. The quality of our service. The quality of our thankfulness. Well, you get the picture. If a real shy introvert challenges themselves to get up in front of an audience to give their testimony of how they became a believer, it counts more with God than when an extrovert who likes to be the center of attention does it. When someone who has been abused as a child by their parent becomes a loving and caring parent, it counts more with God than when the same thing is done by someone with a happy childhood who had great parents. God looks at every one of us as unique and he evaluates our behavior knowing the full measure of where we are coming from and what we have been through. So there is no point in comparing yourself to someone else. To God we are unique and our life story is literally incomparable.

WEEK THIRTEEN

"Jesus wept"

John 11: 35

It is the shortest verse in the entire Bible and yet it says so much about the character of God. So many people have the view that God is uncaring and unemotional. The question "Why God?" is on the lips of at least one person on the planet every single day of the year. Some people view God as something like the Vulcan character of Spock from *Star Trek*. Yet why is this? How has

God gotten so bad of a reputation? I believe it has to do with all the suffering and evil in this world. God created a world of free will and because of that, death and suffering has entered the world. So when Jesus' close friend Lazarus died and he saw the grief of the crowd, he was moved by emotion. Yes, even God cries. When we suffer in this world, Jesus cries along with our own tears. When the crowd saw Jesus crying they said "See how he loved him!", referring to Lazarus. In the same way, you should realize that although you may be going through hard times, God loves you very much.

The evangelist Billy Graham would say repeatedly in his sermons that even if you were the only person alive on earth, Jesus would still have gone to the cross for you. So the next time you feel that God is far away, remember that God is with you.

FIND OUT
WHAT'S NEXT FOR
VICTOR SCOTT
RODRIGUEZ

VISIT www.victorscottrodriguez.com

JOIN his mailing list to learn about events, news and special offers.

LIKE him on Facebook:
Facebook.com/victorscottrodriguez

FOLLOW him on Twitter:
Twitter.com/victorscottrod

PIN him on Pinterest:
Pinterest.com/victorscottrodriguez

FOLLOW him on Instagram:
Instagram.com/victorscottrodriguez

www.ingramcontent.com/pod-product-compliance
Lightning Source LLC
Chambersburg PA
CBHW060052050426
42448CB00011B/2425